Timeless Books of Truth

When you're seeking a book on practical spiritual living, you want to know it's based on an authentic tradition of timeless teachings and resonates with integrity.

This is the goal of Crystal Clarity Publishers: to offer you books of practical wisdom filled with true spiritual principles that have not only been tested through the ages but also through personal experience.

Started in 1968, Crystal Clarity is the publishing house of Ananda, a spiritual community dedicated to meditation and living by true values, as shared by Paramhansa Yogananda, and his direct disciple, Swami Kriyananda, the founder of Ananda. The members of our staff and each of our authors live by these principles. Our worldwide work touches thousands around the world whose lives have been enriched by these universal teachings.

We publish only books that combine creative thinking, universal principles, and a timeless message. Crystal Clarity books will open doors to help you discover more fulfillment and joy by living and acting from the center of peace within you.

How to Be Happy All the Time

All the Time

Paramhansa Yogananda

How to Be Happy All the Time

Paramhansa Yogananda

Crystal Clarity Publishers
Nevada City, California

ISBN: 1-56589-215-1

Printed in Canada
1 3 5 7 9 10 8 6 4 2
Designed by Crystal Clarity Publishers

℗

Crystal Clarity Publishers
14618 Tyler Foote Road
Nevada City, CA 95959
800.424.1055 or 530.478.7600
clarity@crystalclarity.com
www.crystalclarity.com

Library of Congress Cataloging-in-Publication Data

Yogananda, Paramhansa, 1893-1952.
  How to be happy all the time / by Paramhansa Yogananda.
    p. cm.
  ISBN-13: 978-1-56589-215-6 (pbk.)
  1. Happiness--Religious aspects--Self-Realization Fellowship. I. Title.
  BP605.S4Y544 2005
  294.5'44--dc22

                              2005029266

Contents

Publisher's Note

This book offers you simple yet profound secrets for bringing happiness into your life in all circumstances. The thoughts are engaging, practical, and deeply inspiring.

The author, Paramhansa Yogananda, came to the United States from India in 1920, bringing Americans the teachings and techniques of yoga, the ancient science of soul-awakening. He was the first master of yoga to make his home in the West, and his *Autobiography of a Yogi* quickly became a worldwide bestseller, fueling the awakening fascination with Eastern teachings in the West.

Yoga is the ancient science of redirecting one's energies toward spiritual awakening. In addition to bringing Americans the most practical and effective techniques for meditation, Yogananda applied these principles to all areas of life. He showed people how to approach life from a center of inner peace and happiness. He was a prolific writer, lecturer, and composer during the 32 years he lived in America.

The quotations included in this book are taken from many of the lessons he wrote in the 1930s, from *Inner Culture* and *East West* magazines published before 1943, as well as from his original interpretation of *The Rubaiyat* of Omar Khayyam, edited by Swami Kriyananda, and from notes taken by Swami Kriyananda during his years living with Yogananda as a close disciple.

Our goal in this book is to let the Master's spirit come clearly through, with minimal editing. Sometimes sentences have been deleted because of redundancy, sometimes words or punctuation have been changed to clarify the meaning. Most of what is included here is not available elsewhere.

We sincerely hope that Yogananda's words will fill your life with greater peace, fulfillment, and true happiness.

Crystal Clarity Publishers

CHAPTER 1

LOOKING FOR HAPPINESS IN THE WRONG PLACE

To seek happiness outside ourselves is like trying to lasso a cloud. Happiness is not a thing: It is a state of mind. It must be lived. Neither worldly power nor moneymaking schemes can ever capture happiness. Mental restlessness results from an outward focus of awareness. Restlessness itself guarantees that happiness will remain elusive. Temporal power and money are not states of mind. Once obtained, they only dilute a person's happiness. Certainly they cannot enhance it.

The more widely we scatter our energies, the less power we have left to direct toward any specific undertaking. Octopus habits of worry and nervousness rise from ocean depths in the subconscious, fling tentacles around our minds, and crush to death all that we once knew of inner peace.

True happiness is never to be found outside the Self. Those who seek it there are as if chasing rainbows among the clouds!

Like the short-lived roses, countless human beings appear daily in earth's garden. In their youth, they open fresh, hopeful buds, welcoming life's promises and nodding with eager expectancy to every breeze of sense-enjoyment. And then—the petals begin to fade; expectancy turns to disappointment. In the twilight of old age they droop, gray in disillusionment.

Mark the rose's example: Such is the destiny of human beings who live centered in the senses.

Analyze, with understanding born of introspection, the true nature of sense-pleasures. For even as you delight in them, don't you sense in your heart a chilling breath of doubt and uncertainty? You cling to them, yet know in your heart that someday they cannot but betray you.

Closer scrutiny reveals that sense-indulgence actually mocks its votaries. What it offers is not freedom, but soul-bondage. The way of escape lies not, as most people imagine, down moss-soft lanes of further indulgence, but up hard, rocky paths of self-control.

❦

People forget that the price of luxury is an ever-increasing expenditure of nerve and brain energy, and the consequent shortening of their natural life span.

Materialists become so engrossed in the task of making money that they can't relax enough to enjoy their comforts even after they've acquired them.

How unsatisfactory is modern life! Just look at the people around you. Ask yourself, are they happy? See the sad expressions on so many faces. Observe the emptiness in their eyes.

A materialistic life tempts mankind with smiles and assurances, but is consistent only in this: It never fails, eventually, to break all its promises!

※

As a man allows himself to depend increasingly on circumstances outside himself for his physical, mental, and spiritual nourishment, never looking within to his own source, he gradually depletes his reserves of energy.

※

Possession of material riches, without inner peace, is like dying of thirst while bathing in a lake. If material poverty is to be avoided, spiritual poverty is to be abhorred! It is spiritual poverty, not material lack, that lies at the core of all human suffering.

※

The material scientist uses the forces of nature to make the environment of man better and more comfortable. The spiritual scientist uses mind-power to enlighten the soul.

Mind-power shows man the way to inner happiness, which gives him immunity to outer inconveniences.

Of the two types of scientist, which would you say renders the greater service? The spiritual scientist, surely.

※

Pure love, sacred joy, poetic imagination, kindness, wisdom, peace, and happiness are felt *inside* first in the mind or the heart, and are then transmitted through the nervous system to the physical body. Understand and feel the superior joys of the inner life, and you will prefer them to the fleeting pleasures of the outer world.

All physical pleasures arise on the surface of the body and are experienced by the mind through the nervous system. You love the outer pleasures of the senses because you happened to be captured by them first, and then you remained their prisoner. Even as some people get used to jail, so we mortals like the outward pleasures, which shut off the joys from within.

For the most part, the senses promise us a little temporary happiness, but give us sorrow in the end. Virtue and inner happiness do not promise much, but in the end always give lasting happiness. That is why I call the lasting, inner happiness of the soul, "Joy" and the impermanent sense thrills, "Pleasure."

Outer environment and the company you keep are of paramount importance. The specific outer environment of early life is especially important in stimulating or stifling the inner instinctive environment of a child. A child is usually born with a prenatal mental environment. This is stimulated if the outer environment is like the inner environment, but if the outer environment is different from it, the inner environment is likely to be suppressed. An instinctively bad child may be suppressed and made good in good company, and vice versa, while an instinctively good child placed in good company will, no doubt, increase his goodness.

Have you thought seriously why you love fleeting, deceiving pleasures in preference to the lasting peace and joy of the Soul—found so distinctly and ever-increasingly in meditation? It is because in the beginning you happened to cultivate the habit of indulging in sense pleasures and did not cultivate the superior joy of the inner life found in meditation. Understand and feel the superior joys of the inner life, and you will prefer them to the fleeting pleasures of the outer world.

⚜

A man who lived in the cold tracts of Alaska had tasted some of the luscious, lady-finger grapes that had been shipped to him by a friend who lived in Fresno, California. The Alaskan was so enamored of the grapes that he secured a job in Fresno, where all kinds of grapes grow abundantly, and left Alaska for good.

The Alaskan, on his arrival in Fresno, was invited to the house of a friend, and a young lady brought him a bunch of the grapes he so loved. He was almost beside himself with joy, and as he hurriedly munched and gulped down the grapes, he gurgled out: "Oh thank you, from the bottom of my heart, thank you. I left Alaska for lady-finger grapes."

"Well, sir, you shall have all the grapes you want. I am the owner of a grape ranch, and daily I will bring you plenty of grapes," said the lady.

The next day, very early, the lady arrived at the house of the grape-gorged Alaskan with a large quantity of grapes. The Alaskan, who had not yet digested all the grapes he had swallowed the previous night, came out of the house yawning. He leaped with joy at the prospect of feasting on the large amount of grapes the lady had brought.

"Oh, how wonderful to have so many grapes! I am very lucky. Thank you, thank you," cried the Alaskan. He tasted a few grapes in the presence of the lady as a matter of politeness, although he could taste the undigested grapes of the previous night in his mouth. When the lady left, he gloated over the grapes with admiration and greedy eyes. An hour elapsed, then he began eating grapes again. All day long he swallowed grapes, grapes, grapes.

Next morning, at the break of dawn, the young lady arrived with a larger quantity of the finest grapes from her vineyard and shouted for the Alaskan. Half sleepy, with a slightly wilted enthusiasm and a touch of vexation at being roused from a deep sleep, but wearing a gentle smile on his face, the Alaskan greeted the grapes and the lady: "Hello, good lady, thank you for the very nice grapes."

On the third morning, as usual, the lady brought a large bunch of grapes. The Alaskan, half asleep, and with a half smile on his face, greeted the lady and said: "Lady, it is very good of you to give me these grapes, but I still have some left from yesterday."

On the fourth morning, the lady called on the Alaskan again with a good quantity of grapes. He reluctantly woke up, and without a smile greeted the lady and said: "Oh, grapes again. It is very nice of you to bring them, but I have enough."

But the lady, disbelieving the story of the Alaskan and thinking he was just afraid to impose upon her generosity, brought the biggest quantity of grapes on the fifth morning and knocked at the residence of the Alaskan. He leaped out of bed as if he'd seen a ghost and shouted at the lady: "Horrors, lady, grapes, grapes, grapes! For Heaven's sake, grapes again!" The lady smiled and said: "I am happy to know that you hate grapes. I hope you will never deprive me of my salable grapes again."

The above story shows that too much of anything is bad. No matter how pleasurable a thing is, if you over-indulge in it, it ceases to give pleasure and gives pain instead.

So, remember, do not over-indulge in eating, sleeping, working, social activity, or in any activity, no matter how pleasurable it is, for an over-indulgence will yield nothing but unhappiness.

It is important to differentiate between your needs and your wants. Your needs are few, while your wants can be limitless. In order to find freedom and bliss, minister only to your needs. Stop creating limitless wants and pursuing the will-o'-the-wisp of false happiness. The more you depend upon conditions outside yourself for happiness, the less happiness you will experience.

❦

Fostering the desire for luxuries is the surest way to increase misery. Do not be the slave of things or possessions. Boil down even your needs. Spend your time in search of lasting happiness or bliss. The unchangeable, immortal soul is hidden behind the screen of your consciousness, on which are painted dark pictures of disease, failure, death, and so forth. Lift the veil of illusive change and be established in your immortal nature. Enthrone your fickle consciousness on the changelessness and calmness within you, which is the throne of God. Let your soul manifest bliss night and day.

Happiness can be secured by the exercise of self-control, by cultivating habits of plain living and high thinking, and by spending less money, even though earning more. Make an effort to earn more so that you can be the means of helping others to help themselves. One of Life's unwritten laws is that he who helps others to abundance and happiness will always be helped in return, and he will become more and more prosperous and happy. This is a law of happiness which cannot be broken. Is it not better to live simply and frugally and grow rich in reality?

∗

The soul cannot find its lost happiness in material things for the simple reason that the comfort they offer is counterfeit. Having lost contact with divine bliss within, man hopes to satisfy his need for it in the pseudo-pleasures of the senses. On deeper levels of his being, however, he remains aware of his former, supernal state in God. True satisfaction eludes him, for what he seeks, while rushing restlessly from one sense pleasure to another, is his lost happiness in the Lord.

Ah, blindness! How long must you continue before, suffering from satiety, boredom, and disgust, you seek joy within, where alone it can be found?

∗

Think for a moment what Jesus meant when he said, "Let the dead bury their dead." (Matthew 8:22) His meaning was that most people are dead but don't know it! They have no ambition, no initiative, no spiritual enthusiasm, no joy in life.

What is the use of living that way? Life should be a constant inspiration. To live mechanically is to be dead inside though your body be still breathing!

The reason people's lives are so dull and uninteresting is that they depend on shallow channels for their happiness, instead of going to the limitless source of all joy within themselves.

❦

What is the use of spending all one's time on things that don't last? The drama of life has for its moral the fact that it is merely that: a drama, an illusion.

Fools, imagining the play to be real and lasting, weep through the sad parts, grieve that the happy parts cannot endure, and sorrow that the play must, at last, come to an end. Suffering is the punishment for their spiritual blindness.

The wise, however, seeing the drama for the utter delusion it is, seek eternal happiness in the Self within.

CHAPTER 2

HAPPINESS IS A CHOICE

If you want to be sad, no one in the world can make you happy. But if you make up your mind to be happy, no one and nothing on earth can take that happiness from you.

❧

If you have given up hope of ever being happy, cheer up. Never lose hope. Your soul, being the reflection of the ever-joyous Spirit, is happiness itself. If you keep the eyes of your concentration closed, you cannot see the sun of happiness burning within your bosom. But no matter how tightly you close the eyes of your attention, the happiness rays continuously try to pierce the closed doors of your mind. Open the portals of calmness and you will find the bright sun of joy within yourself.

The joyous rays of the soul can be perceived if you interiorize your attention. Do not search for happiness only in beautiful clothes, delicious dinners, and other comforts. These will imprison your happiness behind the bars of outwardness.

If you have made up your mind to find joy within yourself, sooner or later you will find it. Seek it daily, by continuously deeper meditation within, and you will surely find everlasting happiness. Make a steady effort to go within, and you will find your greatest happiness there.

Happiness comes, not by helplessly wishing for it, but by dreaming, thinking, and living it in all circumstances. No matter what you are doing, keep the undercurrent of happiness, the secret river of joy, flowing beneath the sands of your thoughts and the rocky soils of hard trials.

Some people smile most of the time while they hide a sorrow-corroded heart. Such people slowly pine away beneath the shadows of meaningless smiles. There are other people who smile once in a while, yet have beneath the surface a million fountains of laughing peace.

Learn to be secretly happy within your heart in spite of all circumstances, and say to yourself, "Happiness is the greatest divine birthright—the buried treasure of my soul. I have found that I am secretly rich beyond the dream of kings."

Persons of strong character are usually the happiest. They do not blame others for troubles that can be traced to their own actions and lack of understanding. They know that no one has the power to add to their happiness or detract from it, unless they themselves allow the adverse thoughts or wicked actions of others to affect them.

A strong determination to be happy will help you. Do not wait for your situation to change, thinking that therein lies the trouble. Try to be happy under all circumstances. If your happiness sometimes seems dependent on certain conditions, then change your circumstances so that you will be happy all the time.

Don't be bound by set rules, as there are exceptions to every rule. Perhaps you say, "If this or that happens, I shall be very contented." Don't wait. Snatch the highest prize of happiness that is within your reach now, for the will-o'-the-wisp of hoping for happiness, and thereby postponing it, leads you through many sloughs of disappointment.

Happiness grows by what feeds it. Learn to be happy by *being happy all the time.* John said, "If I get money, I shall be happy." After he became wealthy, he said, "I shall be happy if I get rid of my acute indigestion." His indigestion was cured, but he thought, "If I get a wife, I shall be happy." Marriage brought him nothing but unhappiness. His second marriage was worse than the first. He thought that he would be happier if he divorced his second wife, also, so he did. Now, at the age of seventy, he thought, "I shall never be happy unless I can be youthful again." In this way people try, but they never reach their goal of happiness.

Make up your mind that you will be happy whether you are rich or poor, healthy or unhealthy, happily married or unhappily married, young or old, smiling or crying. Don't wait for yourself, your family, or your surroundings to change before you can be happy within yourself. Make up your mind to be happy within yourself, right now, whatever you are, or wherever you are.

⁂

Modern man takes pride in his scientific approach to reality. Let me then make this proposal: that you analyze life itself—in a laboratory, as it were. Americans love to experiment, so why not experiment on yourselves: on your attitudes toward life, on your thoughts and behavior?

Find out what life is, and how human life might be improved. Discover what people most deeply want in life, and what is the best way for them to achieve their hearts' desire. Find what it is they most want to avoid, and how they might, in future, avoid this unwelcome "guest."

In physics and chemistry, if a person wants the right answers he must ask the right questions. The same is true also in life. Try to find out why so many people are unhappy. Then, having understood that, seek the best way of achieving lasting happiness.

Can you make your half-dead rose plant of life bloom again?

We are usually born rich with smiles, youth, strength, beauty, health, mystic aspirations, and swelling hopes. As we live and grow, we begin to lose these riches, and the roses in us begin to fade. Why is this? The rose blooms only to die. Does our happiness come only in order to vanish?

We want to bloom with good actions, fragrant with happiness, and to rest forever with the memories of those who appreciate us. We do not have to die devoured by poverty, sickness, or sorrow.

To guard our rose plant, we must attend to it properly with much watering, feeding, and guarding it from pests and chill. The rose plant of our happiness can grow only on the fertile soil of our peace. It can never grow on hard, unfeeling soil of human mentality. We have to dig constantly into peace with the spade of our good actions. We have to keep our happiness plant well watered with our spirit of love and service. We can only be happy by making others happy.

The real food for the happiness tree can be supplied only through meditation and actual contact with God in daily life. Without our contact with the Infinite source, from which all our human faculties and inspirations spring, we can never grow perfectly and completely.

The worst pests that attack our plant of happiness are lack of the desire to progress, self-satisfaction, and skepticism. The chill of inertia, or lack of definite, constant effort to know the Truth, is the greatest ill from which our happiness plant suffers.

⚕

Be happy, now! If you succeed in finding happiness in your soul, then even though you die tomorrow and join the long procession of departed souls that slowly moves down pillared corridors of centuries, you will always carry with you that priceless treasure. Once soul-happiness is yours, no one will be able to take it from you, however long be your journey toward timelessness and eternity.

⚕

Most people live a life checkered with sadness and sorrow. They do not avoid the actions which lead to suffering and do not follow the ways which lead to happiness. Some people are over-sensitive to sorrow and happiness when they come. They can be crushed by sorrow or overwhelmed by joy, and thus lose their mental balance. There are very few people who, after burning their fingers in the fire of ignorance, learn to avoid misery-making acts.

Many people wish to be happy, yet they never make the effort to adopt the course of action that leads to happiness. Most people keep rolling down the hill of life, only *mentally* wishing to climb the peak of happiness. They sometimes wake up, if their enthusiasm for happiness survives the crash to the bottom of unhappiness. Most people lack imagination and never wake up until something terrible happens to arouse them from their nightmare of folly.

People seeking happiness must avoid the influence of bad habits that lead to evil actions. Evil actions eventually produce misery that corrodes the body, mind, and soul like a silently burning acid. This misery cannot be long endured and should be strictly avoided.

Cure yourself of evil habits by cauterizing them with the opposite good habits. If you have a bad habit of telling lies, start the opposite good habit of telling the truth. It takes time to form either a good habit or a bad one. It is difficult for a bad person to be good, and for a good person to be bad. Once you become good, it will be natural and easy for you to be good; similarly, if you cultivate an evil habit, you will be compelled to be evil in spite of your desire to be good.

Remember: No matter how much you are accustomed to being unhappy, you must adopt the antidote of happiness. Each act of being happy will help you cultivate the habit of always being happy. Pay no attention if your mind tells you that you can never be happy. Just remember to start being happy now, and every moment say, "I am happy now!" If you can continuously do that, then, when you look back, you can say, "I have been very happy." When you look at yourself now, you will say, "I am happy," and when you look ahead, you will say, "I know I shall be happy." All your future happiness depends upon how happy you are now, so start being happy NOW.

❧

After bathing yourself in the ocean of peace in the dreamland, awake with happiness and say, "In sleep I found myself free from mortal worries. I was a king of peace. Now, as

I work in the daytime and carry on my battles of duties, I will no longer be defeated by rebellious worries of the kingdom of wakefulness. I am a king of peace in the dreamland, and I shall continue to be a king in the land of wakefulness. As I come out of my kingdom of peace in the dreamland, I will spread that same peace in my land of wakeful dreams."

⚘

Happiness depends to some extent upon external conditions, but chiefly upon conditions of the inner mind. In order to be happy, one needs good health, an efficient mind, a prosperous life, the right work and, above all, an all-accomplishing wisdom. A man cannot be happy just by holding the inner calm while completely ignoring the struggle for existence and the effort for success.

But without internal happiness, one can be a prisoner of worries in a rich castle. Happiness does not depend upon success and wealth alone, but upon struggling against the difficulties of life with an acquired attitude of unshakable inner happiness.

To be unhappy as you seek happiness defeats its own end. Happiness comes by being internally happy first, at all times, while struggling your utmost to uproot the causes of unhappiness.

The habit of preserving an internal happy attitude of mind should have been started when you were very young, but it is not too late to begin now. From today onward, make up your mind that when you meet your trying relatives, when you come in contact with your overbearing boss, and when you contact the trials of life, you will try to retain your internal calmness and happiness.

If you persist in carrying out this resolution despite all challenges, you will find that happiness depends upon right mental habit and upon resolving to be happy in all circumstances.

When you learn to be happy at all times, however, do not allow this independent attitude of inner happiness to make you lazy. Do not ignore the material causes that stand in the way of your happiness. Strive to remove them, and go through all the activities of life with this calm, happy attitude of mind.

≫⊱

You must be very joyous and happy, for this is God's dream. The little man and the big man are only projections of the Dreamer's consciousness. Take everything as it comes, and tell yourself that it is all coming from God. What comes of itself, let it come. Even when you feel you have to try to correct a wrong, try first to feel His inner guidance. Then when you act, do so on His behalf, and never with ego-inspired indignation.

CHAPTER 3

AVOIDING THE HAPPINESS THIEVES

Evil is the absence of true joy. That is what makes it evil, you see. Otherwise, can you say that a tiger commits evil in killing its prey? To kill is the tiger's nature, given to it by God. Nature's laws are impersonal.

Evil comes into the picture when one has the potential for attaining inner joy. Anything that separates us from that divine state of being is evil for us, because it distances our awareness from that which we really are, and from that which we really want in life.

Hence the scriptural injunctions against lust, for example, and pride. The commandments are for man's welfare, not for the Lord's gratification! They are warnings to the unwary, that, although certain attitudes and actions may at first seem fulfilling, the end of the road for anyone pursuing them is not happiness, but pain.

People seeking happiness must avoid the influence of bad habits which lead to evil actions. Evil actions produce misery sooner or later.

The repetition of a few weak actions produces habits of weakness. Most people allow their self-created habits of weakness or failure to enslave them. You can save yourself if you have made up your mind to live differently, but your resolution to fight bad habits must be persistent until success is reached.

Whatever you made yourself in the past, that is what you are now. It is you, who, by the secret, invisible traces of your own past actions, have been controlling the power of your present actions.

It is you who, through the law of cause and effect that governs your actions, ordered yourself to be punished or rewarded. You have probably suffered enough. It is time now for you to parole yourself from the prison of your own past undesirable habits. Since you are the judge, no jail of suffering, poverty, or ignorance can hold you if you are ready to liberate yourself.

❧

Avoid speaking negative things. Why look at the drains, when there is beauty all around? You could take me into the most perfect room in the world, and still, if I wanted to, I would be able to find faults in it. But why should I want to? Why not enjoy its beauty?

If we concentrate on the bad side, we lose sight of the good. Doctors say that millions of terrible germs pass through our bodies. But because we aren't aware of them they are far less likely to affect us than if we sensed their presence, and worried about it. When we look at the negative side long enough, we ourselves take on negative qualities. When we concentrate on the good, we take on goodness.

Worries are hard to eliminate. You kill off some and others seem to swarm in seemingly from nowhere. They almost bite the life out of you. Just as you use ant poison to kill the pests that infest your house, so you must use the chemical of peace to destroy thoughts of worry. Every time a swarm of worries invades you, refuse to be bothered, and wait calmly, seeking the remedy. Spray the appearing worries with your powerful peace chemical.

You cannot buy this peace chemical in any drug store. You must manufacture it in the stillness of your daily practice of concentration. This peace chemical is a compound of the burning acids of habitual calmness and sorrow-killing pale happiness. The acids of calmness and pale happiness must be prepared in the laboratory of self-discipline and constant trials.

Worries are stupefied by calmness and slight happiness, but are completely eradicated by the constant culture of steadfast peace. Worries can't be quelled by more worrying or by madly racing to quell them, but all worry-pests can be destroyed by the habit of fostering powerful peace.

⚜

Beware! The mind must be protected from the four alternating psychological states of sorrow, false happiness, indifference, and a deceptive, passive peace that claims the ego for brief intervals, whenever it manages to shake off the other three. Look at any face and you will be able to tell whether its owner is at the mercy of any one of these. Rarely do people's faces remain calm while they are in the grip of the four unstable mental states.

Whenever a person is denied his desire for something like health or pleasure, sorrow comes and changes that person's face. "Prince Smile" is routed by "King Sadness," who tortures the muscles and distorts the expression.

Whenever a person's desire is fulfilled, he is temporarily "happy." Sorrow is born of unfulfilled desire; "happiness," of fulfilled desire. Sorrow and false happiness, like Siamese twins, dwell and travel together. They are the children of desire and are never far apart; if you invite false happiness, sorrow is sure to follow.

When the ego is not buffeted about by sorrow or "happiness," people find themselves in the third state: indifference or boredom.

You ask a person engrossed in indifference, "Are you sad?"

"Oh no," he replies.

Then you ask him, "Are you happy?"

"Oh no," he drawls.

"Well then," you ask, "what is the matter with you?"

"Oh," he cries, "I am just bored."

That is the mental state of many people.

Beyond these changeable states of sorrow, false happiness, and indifference lies the neutral state of passive mental peace. It is of a negative, short-lived nature—the aftermath of, and temporary lull in, the first-mentioned three states.

Beyond these four states of consciousness is the unconditional, ever-new state of Bliss felt only in meditation.

❀

Don't spend too much time joking. I myself like to laugh, but I have my sense of humor under control. When I am serious, nobody can tempt me to laugh. Be happy and cheerful within—grave, but ever cheerful. Why waste your spiritual perceptions in useless words? When you have filled the bucket of your consciousness with the milk of peace, keep it that way; don't drive holes in it with joking and idle speech.

❧

Don't joke too much. Joking is a false stimulant. It doesn't spring from true happiness, and doesn't give true happiness. When you joke a lot, the mind becomes restless and light so that it can't meditate.

❧

Don't make unhappiness a chronic habit, for it is anything but pleasant to be unhappy, and it is blessedness for yourself and others if you are happy. It is easy to wear a silver smile or pour sweet happiness through your voice. Then why be grouchy and scatter unhappiness around you? It is never too late to learn. You are as old as your chronic thoughts, and you are as young as you feel now, in spite of your age.

When Mr. Sorrow comes, do not give him strength by acknowledging his presence. If you feed him with the nectar of your tears, he will stay. He will soon spread all over the bedroom of your life. The minute he arrives, laugh at him — that will cheat him of his joy. Then kick him in the stomach. Apply the fists, limbs, and elbows of your will, and throw him entirely out of the chamber of your life. Thus you will win both a physical and a metaphysical victory over sorrow.

One who was born disadvantaged in any way should resist fiercely the temptation to wallow in self-pity. To feel sorry for oneself is to dilute one's inner power to overcome.

Your individual happiness depends to a large extent upon protecting yourself and your family from the evil results of gossiping. See no evil, speak no evil, hear no evil, think no evil, feel no evil. Most people can talk about other people for hours and thrive under the influence of gossip, like the temporary influence of intoxicating, poisonous wine. Isn't it strange that people can smoothly, joyously, and with caustic criticism talk about the faults of others for hours, but cannot endure reference to their own faults at all?

The next time you are tempted to talk about the moral and mental wickedness of other people, immediately begin to talk loudly about your own mental and moral wickedness for just five minutes and see how you like it. If you do not like to talk about your own faults, if it hurts you to do so, you certainly should feel more hurt when saying unkind and harmful things about other people. Train yourself, and each member of your family, to refrain from talking about others.

By giving publicity to a person's weakness, you do not help him. Instead, you either make him wrathful or discouraged, and you shame him, perhaps forever, so that he gives up trying to be good. When you take away the sense of dignity from a person by openly maligning him, you make him desperate.

When a man is down, he is too well aware of his own wickedness. By destructive criticism, you push him still farther down into the mire of despondency into which he is already sinking. Instead of gossiping about him, you should pull him out with loving, encouraging words. Only when aid is asked should spiritual and moral help be offered. To your own children or loved ones, you may offer your friendly, humble suggestions at any time and remove their sense of secrecy or delicacy.

"Judge not, that ye be not judged. For with what judgment ye judge, ye shall be judged; and with what measure ye mete, it shall be measured to you again." (Matthew 7:1-2) There is plenty of dirt to remove from your own mental home. Do not indulge in evil talk about the mental dirt in the lives of other people, but get busy and free your own life from weaknesses. Silently heal yourself of the desire to criticize, and when free from condemnation and gossip yourself, teach others to be better by your sympathetic heart and good example.

❦

Unkind words used in a fit of emotion are like a conflagration that spreads over the forest of friendship and burns up all the green plants of courteous dealings and sympathetic thoughts.

People drunk with excitement and accustomed to anger-slavery are emotional firebugs who, at the slightest provocation, light the matches of wrathful words and set fire to the inner peace of souls.

As forest fires cause millions of dollars of loss to the country, so emotional firebugs, by setting fire to the happiness of millions of intelligent people, cause billions of dollars of loss to creative thinking, and cause great waste of human nerve-energy.

In order to be kind, it is not necessary to agree about everything. If you disagree, always remain calm and courteous. It is human weakness to get angry and scold, but it is divine strength to hold the reins of your temper and speech. No matter what provokes you, behave yourself. By calm silence, or by genuine kind words, show that your kindness is more powerful than the other person's ugliness. Before the mellow light of your forgiveness, all the gathered hatred of your enemies will melt away.

If you are suffering from the indigestion of unkindness or crabbiness, drink the medicine of sweetness. If you make up your mind to change, start by speaking sincere, kind words to those to whom you have been unjustly harsh. First, be courteous to your immediate relatives. When you can do that, you will be habitually kind to all people. Happiness has its foundation on the altar of understanding and kind words.

Unkind words are ruthless murderers of lifelong friend-ships and the harmony of homes. Banish unkind words from your lips forever, and make your home life safe from trouble. Sincere, sweet words are nectar to thirsty souls.

They are in demand everywhere. Sweet words create happiness in friends, enemies, churches, business offices, and everywhere. People feel happy when a crabby person leaves the room, and they are glad when a sweet-voiced, sincere friend appears.

※

People are afraid of decaying diseases that beset the body. But few seriously hunt for a cure when they contract the dread psychological disease of jealousy. Shakespeare called it a canker eating at the roots of love. It is worse than that.

The jealousy epidemic seems to be raging in the minds of all nationalities. Jealousy is the matrimonial TB. It eats into happy, healthy married life and utterly destroys it by hemorrhages of suspicion. Continuous mutual nagging acts like bronchial outbursts, affecting the lungs of happiness.

It is also the business tuberculosis. When it enters into a business concern, the tissues of cooperation and unity, which are the life of an organization, begin slowly or rapidly to decay. All healthful political and religious organizations should beware of this decaying disease. Guard your happiness from its devastation.

❧

If you are a slave to your senses, you cannot be happy. If you are a master of your desires and appetites, you can be a really happy person. If you overeat against your will; if you wish anything contrary to your conscience; if you act wrongly, forced by your senses, against the wish of your Inner Self, then you cannot be happy. People who are slaves to the senses find that their evil habits compel them to do things that will hurt them. Stubborn bad habits bludgeon your will power every time it tries to take the lead and guide your thoughts to the kingdom of right action. The remedy lies in rescuing your will power from the imprisoning power of the senses.

To yield to bad habits is to make them stronger and your will power weaker. Fight your bad habits of anger, fault-finding, jealousy, fear, inertia, overeating, or whatever your particular weakness is, by not yielding to temptation against your will. When you determine to do something that you know is absolutely right, go through with it at any cost. This will give your wisdom-guided will more power over your bad habits. Renounce last year's material failure, spiritual indifference, mental and moral weaknesses, and half-hearted meditations by using your will to be prosperous, by exercising self-control, and by meditating deeply until you actually contact God.

Almost every soul is a prisoner of the senses, which are entrenched on the surface of the body. The soul's attention is lured away from its inner kingdom in the medulla, the spiritual eye, and the chakras, to the outer regions of the body, where greed, temptation, and attachment have their strongholds. The devotee who wants to lead King Soul away from the misery-making slums of the senses, finds that he cannot do so without a severe clash between the soldiers of the senses and the divine soldiers of the Soul.

❦

If you haven't enough will power, try to develop *won't* power. When you are at the dinner table and Mr. Greed lures you to eat more than you should, and tries to chloroform your self-control and cast you into the pit of indigestion — watch yourself. After partaking of the right quality and quantity of food, just say to yourself, "I won't eat any more," and get up from the table and run. When somebody calls, "John, come back and eat some more. Don't forget the delicious apple pie," just call back, "I *won't*."

Thoughts of dishonesty, temptation, or revengefulness are soldiers of the misery-making senses. They want to conquer the kingdom of your happiness and keep you prisoner in the dungeon of unhappiness and misery. As soon as the soldiers of wrong thoughts rally together to attack your inner peace, wake up the soul soldiers of light, honesty, and self-control, and wage a furious battle.

Remember, it rests with you whether you want greed, sense-slavery, anger, hatred, revengefulness, or worries to rule your life, or whether you will let the divine soldiers of self-control, calmness, love, forgiveness, peace, and harmony rule your mental kingdom. Drive away the rebel sense habits that have brought misery to the empire of your peace. Be king of yourself, and let the soldiers of goodness and good habits rule the kingdom of your mind. Then happiness will reign within you forever.

⚘

Give both the good and the bad that you do to God. Of course, that does not mean you should deliberately do things that are bad, but when you cannot help yourself because of too-strong habits, feel that God is acting through you. Make *Him* responsible. He likes that! For He wants you to realize that it is He who is dreaming your existence.

⚘

As long as you are making the effort, God will *never* let you down!

CHAPTER 4

LEARN TO BEHAVE

Never can I thank my teacher enough for constantly saying to me, "Learn to behave."

I discovered I could see myself reflected more clearly through others' minds, especially through my Master's unprejudiced mind, than through my own hazy understanding.

I began to associate with calm minds and to ask them how I looked from their mental perceptions, for I found there was a difference between what I thought others thought of me and what others *actually* thought of me in their inner minds.

It takes a lot of courage to risk a word battle, or other trouble, just for telling people their faults. That is why most people are afraid to criticize you to your face. Most people bite you behind your back and silently criticize you in their own minds.

Your intimate friends do not criticize you openly for fear of offending you; but they criticize you inwardly, as you do them. If you want to know what your friends think about you, behave perfectly and keep constantly improving yourself by being unselfish, wise, calm, meditative, fearless, sweet, sincere, courteous, methodical, true to your word, and unafraid to be firm, and your friends will be so overwhelmed by your goodness that they will think, and talk loudly, about what you are.

Learn to make yourself behave and be happy, and you will influence all the people you meet to be well behaved and happy.

≈

Self-control at first produces unhappiness because of the separation from the pleasure-yielding senses. After self-control ripens, however, the soul begins to experience finer, happier perceptions and to enjoy itself far more than when it lived identified with the sense-pleasures. The devotee, suffering from fear of the feeling of emptiness, must realize that renunciation is not an end in itself. Rather, it is a means to an end, and teaches one to shift the attention from lesser sense-pleasures to deeper soul pleasures.

≈

Never dwell on the thought of your shortcomings. Recall, instead, the memory of the good things you have done, and of the goodness that exists in the world. Convince yourself of your own innate perfection. Thus you will find

yourself drawn to remember your eternal nature as a child of
God.

❧

The only worthwhile accomplishments are not those we
achieve outwardly, but the victories we win over ourselves.
Let us create inner dwellings of beautiful qualities, erecting
them in valleys of humbleness where gather the rains of
God's mercy and of other people's good wishes for us.

Divine grace can make fertile the most arid heart, trans-
forming its brown desert into a verdant garden of inner
happiness and peace.

❧

If you want to be loved, start loving others who need
your love. If you expect others to be honest with you, then
start by being honest yourself. If you want others to sympa-
thize with you, start showing sympathy to those around you.
If you want to be respected, you must learn to be respectful
to everyone, both young and old. If you want a display of
peace from others, you must be peaceful yourself. If you
want others to be religious, start being spiritual yourself.

Whatever you want others to be, first be that yourself. Then, you will find others responding in like manner to you.

It is easy to wish that others would behave perfectly toward you, and it is easy to see their faults, but it is very difficult to conduct yourself properly and to consider your own faults. If you can remember to behave rightly, others will try to follow your example. If you can find your own faults without developing an inferiority complex, and can keep busy correcting yourself, then you will be using your time more profitably than if you spend it wishing others were better. Your good example will do more to change others than your wishing, your wrath, or your words.

The more you improve yourself, the more you will elevate others around you and the happier you will become. The happier you become, the happier will be the people around you.

Stagnant people are unhappy. Extremely ignorant people scarcely know how it feels to be either happy or unhappy. It is better to be unhappy about your own ignorance than to die happily with it. Wherever you are, remain awake and alive with your thought, perception, and intuition—ever ready to appreciate exemplary conduct and to ignore bad behavior. Your highest happiness lies in being ever ready to learn and to behave properly.

Most bored people who think they have exhausted the joys of life do not know that a world of solace lies in good books. The vacant mind is the workshop of worry and despair. In choosing books, the first preference should be given to spiritual books that are free from dogma. In studying, you must master one subject or more, but you should also know something of every other subject, including botany, logic, astronomy, music, languages, and politics. The study of physiology is important. Read a good scientific magazine every month.

Reading is the best indoor intellectual sport. It keeps your mind busy and your intellect exercised. One or two hours' daily reading will give any person a liberal education in ten years, if he chooses worthwhile books. Don't waste time and injure your mental faculties by reading purposeless or trashy books. Not to cultivate a genuine interest in books is to miss the heritage of the ages.

If you cannot get along with friends and the world, read books and keep company with those silent friends who have the power to comfort and inspire. Those who are socially inclined will find a new power to help humanity through the lessons of books written by noble and gifted people.

Read, mark, and inwardly digest selected passages from great books. Discuss important topics with intelligent people. Logically thinking over a given idea is the best way to develop originality in your ideas. When thinking, keep your eyes closed and your mind wholly concentrated on the subject of your study. Do nothing with only half-attention or half-heartedly.

Good books are your perpetual silent friends. When you are worried or grieved, take a book and bury yourself in it. Listen to the comforting and inspiring words of the great minds of the ages.

❧

If you read spiritual books, choose those that contain Self-realization. Such books as the Bible and the Bhagavad Gita should not be read as you would read a novel. Read a passage, think about its meaning, and meditate on its truth. Then try to live the truth in life.

There are three Bibles from which I draw my inspiration: the Christian Bible, the Hindu Bhagavad Gita, and my *Whispers from Eternity*, which were given to me by God. Through meditation and intuitive perception I get more intellectual truths than through reading books.

Read books after meditation. Criticize books with intuitive perception. Keep your mind busy most of the time with good books unless you are meditating. In your spare time, keep busy reading interesting books, which protect your mind from idle thoughts that create boredom and dissatisfaction.

Husband and wife should balance their love by self-control and by reading and discussing good books together, instead of by engaging their minds in fruitless family wars or peace-devastating matrimonial skirmishes.

❦

If you want to be happy, learn to live alone and to plunge into introspection about every experience—good books, problems, religion, philosophy, and inner happiness. Contented, self-chosen, habitual seclusion is the price of real happiness. When you are forced into a crowd of talkers, retire within the cell of your deep thoughts and enjoy the peace of your inner fountain of silence.

❦

Don't joke too much. I, myself, as you know, like a good laugh, but if I make up my mind to be serious, no one can make me even smile. Be happy and cheerful—above all inwardly. Be outwardly grave, but inwardly cheerful.

Don't waste the perception of God's presence, acquired in meditation, by useless chatting. Idle words are like bullets: they riddle the milk pail of peace. In devoting time unnecessarily to conversation and exuberant laughter, you'll find you have nothing left inside. Fill the pail of your consciousness with the milk of meditative peace, then keep it filled. Joking is false happiness. Too much laughter riddles the mind and lets the peace in the bucket flow out, wasting it.

Meditate regularly, and you will find a joy inside that is real. You will then have something you can compare to sense pleasures. That comparison will automatically make you want to forsake your sorrow-producing bad habits. The best way to overcome temptation is to have something more fulfilling with which to compare it.

❦

Never let your mind be seduced by restlessness, through joking too much, too many distractions, and so on. Be deep. As soon as you succumb to restlessness, all the old troubles will begin to exert their pull on the mind once again: sex, wine, and money.

Of course, a little fun and laughter is good, occasionally. But don't let light-mindedness possess you. I, too, like to laugh sometimes, as you know. But when I choose to be serious, nothing and no one can draw me out of my inner Self.

Be deep in everything you do. Even when laughing, don't lose your inner calmness. Be joyful inside, but always inwardly a little withdrawn. Be centered in the joy within.

Dwell always in the Self. Come down a little bit when you have to, to eat, or talk, or to do your work; then withdraw into the Self again.

Be calmly active, and actively calm. That is the way of the yogi.

∗

When a cloudy day comes, think of the clusters of sunny days that you have had. When the blues come and make you feel they are going to take a permanent lease on your life, think of the numberless days of happiness which you have enjoyed in the past. It is ingratitude to the Giver of all gifts to forget the healthy smiles enjoyed for fifty years just because you have been sick for six months. There is no sense in unbalancing your mind and forgetting years of happiness by taking too seriously the sorrows of a few weeks or a few months.

Be not afraid of this temporary mortal ignorance, for within your soul lies buried the unopened mine of the wisdom of God. Since you are made in His image, all His wisdom and happiness lie hidden somewhere in the disorganized cellar of your subconsciousness. To smile when all things are going well is easy and natural, but to smile when all things try to ruin you is difficult, superconscious, admirable, and the harbinger of lasting happiness. Become a smile specialist and a doctor of blues, healing all the sad and weary hearts you meet by the x-ray of your smiles.

When you are sick, do not concentrate on the length of your suffering, but dream about the youthful, healthful years you have already enjoyed. What you have had, you can have again if you try hard enough. To give up is the difficult, miserable way in the long run; to try hard until you succeed is the easiest way.

Banish sadness with joy; destroy sickening thoughts of failure with the tonic of success consciousness. Polish disharmony with the chisel of harmony. Cauterize worries with calmness. Cast sorrows into the flames of happiness.

Shame unkindness by kindness. Dethrone sick thoughts and place King Vitality on the throne of right living. Banish restlessness and ignorance from the shores of your mind. Establish the kingdom of silence within, and the God of happiness will freely enter.

CHAPTER 5

SIMPLICITY IS THE KEY

Simplicity is not grinding poverty: It is not the polar opposite of wealth. To live simply is to pursue a quiet path of moderation. In a life of balance between opposite extremes lies inner happiness.

True lovers, at peace with themselves and with the world around them, accepting happily whatever comes their way, are justified in pitying the very lot of kings.

Happiness is mankind's true and native state of being. Few people find it, for most of them live at their periphery; they extend themselves as far as possible from their center within. The richer and more powerful they become, the emptier they feel inwardly.

In kings, the desire for happiness is frustrated more often than fulfilled. Their natural craving for friendship is swept to sea on a daily tide of favor-seekers. Their hope for human understanding is submerged and pounded by a surf of competition for their notice. The greater the crowds surrounding a king, the greater is his inner sense of loneliness.

People everywhere, in their quest for happiness outside themselves, discover in the end that they've been seeking it in an empty cornucopia, and sucking feverishly at the rim of a crystal glass into which was never poured the wine of joy.

Happiness consists in making the mightiest efforts to reduce your desires and needs, and in cultivating the ability to meet those needs at will, always trying to smile, both outwardly and inwardly, in spite of every predicament.

Be silent and calm every night for at least ten minutes (longer if possible) before you retire, and again in the morning before rising. This will produce an undaunted, unbreakable inner habit of happiness that will make you able to meet all the trying situations of the everyday battle of life. With that unchangeable happiness within, go about seeking to fulfill the demands of your day.

Seek happiness more in your mind and less in the acquisition of things. Be so happy in your mind that nothing that comes can possibly make you unhappy. Then, you can get along without things you have been accustomed to. Be happy knowing you have acquired the power not to be negative. Know, too, that you will never again become so materially minded that you forget your inner happiness, even if you become a millionaire.

❧

There are so many things here in America that I wanted for my own impoverished country. In time, however, I found that the people here are not so happy, on average, as the peasants in India—many of whom cannot afford more than one meal a day. Despite the material prosperity here, people haven't the same inner happiness. Americans are satiated with a plethora of sense pleasures. Happiness eludes them for the simple reason that they seek it everywhere except in themselves.

⁂

Most so-called "happiness" is nothing but suffering in disguise. You may enjoy eating a huge meal, but you are also likely to have unpleasant after-effects, such as acute indigestion or stomachache. The greatest way to create happiness for yourself is not to allow sense lures or bad habits to control you, but to be a stern ruler of your habits and appetites. Just as you cannot satisfy your own hunger by feeding another person, so you cannot find happiness in satisfying the over-demands of your senses.

Too much luxury, instead of producing happiness, drives it away from your mind. Do not spend all your time looking for things to make you happy. Be contented always, equally in your struggle for prosperity and in your attainment of it. You can be a King of Happiness in a tattered cottage, or you can be a tortured victim of unhappiness in a palace. Happiness is a mental phenomenon exclusively. You must first establish it firmly within yourself and then, with an undying resolution always to be happy, go through the world seeking health, prosperity, and wisdom.

You will find greater happiness if you seek success ever with a happy attitude than if you try to gain your heart's desire with an unhappy mind, no matter what that desire may be.

❧

It is easier to spend than to earn. It is harder to save than to earn. Most people spend more than they earn. The extra money is acquired by borrowing, or by buying with promises to pay in the future. You must not always feel that you have to "keep up with the Joneses." To try to own more than your purse allows is to live in constant mental worry. To spend more than you earn is to live in perpetual slavery.

Along with the art of money making, it is well to learn the art of money saving. A large income is of no lasting good to you if it only creates habits of luxury with no savings in reserve. Think for a moment: If you should get sick suddenly, how would you continue without the usual income, if you have no savings put away? It is a bad thing to cultivate luxurious habits if you have only a small income. Is it not better to live simply and frugally and grow rich in reality? You should use one-fourth of your income on plain living, save three-fourths, and be at ease in your mind with a feeling of future security. Keep what you earn legitimately, and don't gamble or lose it in trying to "get rich quick."

Happiness can be had by the exercise of self-control, by cultivating habits of plain living and high thinking, by spending less even though earning more. Make an effort to earn more so that you can help others to help themselves.

❦

Joy is too delicate a flower to bloom in the sooted atmosphere of worldly minds, which crave happiness from money and possessions. Joy wilts, too, when people water it inadequately by placing conditions on their happiness, telling themselves, "I won't be really happy until I get that car (or dress, or house, or vacation by the sea)!" Materialistic people, however frantically they pursue the butterfly of happiness, never succeed in catching it. Were they to possess everything their hearts ever craved, happiness would still elude them.

On the other hand, happiness blooms naturally in the hearts of those who are inwardly free. It flows spontaneously, like a mountain spring after April showers, in minds that are contented with simple living and that willingly renounce the clutter of unnecessary, so-called "necessities"— the dream castles of a restless mind.

When a person renounces outward ambition to seek peace within himself, he may feel a certain, fleeting nostalgia for his old, familiar habits. Accustomed as he was formerly to outward busy-ness, simplicity may strike him at times, in the beginning, as stark and unattractive.

Gradually, however, if he perseveres, he will accustom himself to the inner world, and will discover increasing happiness in soul-sufficiency. He will come to appreciate more and more deeply the meaning of true happiness.

One may, similarly, experience a temporary sense of loss after failing in his worldly endeavors. Life then, at first, may seem devoid of any herbage of hope. If, however, after wandering in that desert for a time, he determines to face his new circumstances courageously, he will come to realize that life has not changed essentially at all; that whatever occurred to him was only defined as failure by his own imagination. He may then remember happier moments: the simple delights, for example, that he enjoyed as a child. Suddenly he will understand that inner contentment is itself the one and only valid definition of success—and, quite as wonderfully, that contentment is the one thing in his life he need never lose!

In every case, the wilderness of apparent loss, failure, and disappointment can be coaxed to bloom again, like a barren desert after abundant rain. Newly flowering meadows of peace appear suddenly in minds that seek rest within. The soul then knows a happiness more precious than the greatest success attainable through worldly pursuits.

If you, dear reader, should ever slip, or even fall, from the ladder of success, and find yourself abandoned by wealth and honor, and forced to live in humble circumstances—grieve not. Welcome, rather, the new adventure that life has placed before you.

If your dreams lie in ruin all about you, bravely adjust to your altered circumstances. In simplicity you will find—even if you never sought it there!—the sweet happiness your heart has always craved.

Life will give you more than you ever dreamed, if only you will define prosperity anew: not as worldly gain, but as inner, divine contentment.

CHAPTER 6

SHARING YOUR HAPPINESS WITH OTHERS

Your desire to be happy must include others' happiness.

❧

When we serve others, we serve ourselves. Do not think, "I will help others"—think rather, "I will help *my own, my world*, because I cannot otherwise be happy."

❧

The law of life is designed to teach us how to live in harmony with objective Nature and with our true, inner nature.

If you touch your fingers to a hot stove, they will be burned. The pain you feel will be a warning, put there by Nature to protect you from injuring your body.

And if you treat others unkindly, you will receive unkindness in return, both from others and from life. Your own heart, moreover, will grow shriveled and dry. Thus does Nature warn people that by unkindness they do violence to their attunement with the inner Self.

When we know what the law is and conduct ourselves accordingly, we live in lasting happiness, good health, and perfect harmony with ourselves and with all life.

❧

A few years ago, I had a fine musical instrument, an esraj from India. I loved to play devotional music on it. But a visitor one day admired it. Unhesitatingly I gave it to him. Years later someone asked me, "Weren't you just a little sorry?" "Never for a moment!" I replied. Sharing one's happiness with others only expands one's own happiness.

❧

A lover and beloved can find happiness in each other if they live simple lives, not burdening their existence with opulence, artificiality, and hard-driving ambition.

❧

When two selfish individuals become formally united in matrimony, they will still be separated mentally as long as each of them is walled in by self-love. Locked in prison cells of selfishness, they never achieve happiness and harmony together. In loving, not in being loved, lies the key that will unlock the doors of their hearts and bring them wedded happiness.

Self-love is self-confining. When couples learn to expand their sympathies, and give up limiting them to themselves — whether individually, or to themselves as a couple or a family — they may transform their relationship, and the emotional disharmony that selfishness has produced, into a relationship of selfless, divine love.

Selfless love is the key. Couples that at first defined their relationship in terms of "me and thee," later, with the growth of understanding, learn to think unitively. Human love, thus, can expand into the love of God.

Without God, human love is never perfect. No marriage is truly fruitful without the "secret ingredient" of divine love. Earthly love that reaches not past the beloved to embrace divinity is not real love at all. It is ego-worship, selfish because rooted in desire.

True love emanates from God. Only hearts that have been purified by self-expansion can embrace the fullness of that love. In expansion, the heart's feelings become channels through which God's love flows out to all the world.

❦

People who actually do find happiness in marriage don't find their happiness from one another. Always, it comes from inside themselves. How sad it is to see the suffering people go through, just because they base their expectations of happiness in other people!

❦

Swami Kriyananda describes the following experience:

A congregation member of one of the Self-Realization Fellowship churches came to Paramhansa Yogananda troubled by doubt. "Master," she said, "some people claim that, with so much suffering in the world, it is wrong for anyone to be happy. Doesn't personal enjoyment imply a lack of compassion for the sufferings of others?

"Jesus," she added, "is often depicted as a 'man of sorrows.' I've never heard him described as a man of joy."

Paramhansa Yogananda replied: "The Jesus I know is bliss-filled, and not sorrowful! He grieves for the sorrows of mankind, yes, but his grief doesn't make him grief-stricken.

"Were he actually to embrace others' sorrows, what would he have to give them, except an increase of their misery?

"God's bliss makes those who have it compassionate for the millions who have missed the point of their existence. But compassion only adds to their inner bliss; it doesn't diminish it. For bliss is the cure all men are seeking, whether consciously or unconsciously. It is not a side issue, unrelated to suffering. The more blissful one feels within, the more he longs to share his bliss with all.

"Divine joy comes with self-expansion. Suffering, on the other hand, is the fruit of selfishness, of a contractive ego. Joy awakens compassion in the heart. It makes one long to infuse divine bliss into those who are weeping in sorrow."

❧

Happiness itself, though a universal good, must never be imposed on others; in fact, it never can be. Reforms, if not undertaken in keeping with the divine will, create disharmony.

The good that we do must also be offered with love and respect for the free will of others. Our respect for them should be, above all, for the divine within them. Charity must never deprive its recipients of their divine dignity. When giving, we should encourage others to give at least something in return. We should make them feel our gratitude, too, for their assistance. They will not be benefited if they are made to receive our kindness passively.

※

When a diamond cutter wants to produce a beautiful stone, he knows that he must cut it along its natural cleavage. His cut must not be random, to satisfy some abstract fancy of his own. The same is true for bringing out the beauty in human nature: We must take into account the realities of others, and never seek to impose on them our own.

※

As a person advances spiritually, and discovers joy and divine insight within himself, he naturally wishes that he could find ways to bring his glowing sense of happiness and well-being to all mankind. Yet he learns soon enough that he must deal with things as they are. Mental instability of any kind, for example—and sorrow is a kind of mental imbalance—must be cured sensitively, often gradually, lest too sudden a shock, even of joy, aggravate, and not cure, the disturbance.

It is right and good that each of us do his best to make this world a better place to live in. God is not pleased with selfishness. If a devotee hoards selfishly even the grace he receives in meditation, he gives power to his ego, not to his soul. It may not always be possible for us to accomplish quickly, or easily, our altruistic ends. This fact should not deter us from doing what good we can. Made in the image of God as all of us are, we have potentially within us His hidden power. Let us then live and work from a sense of His guidance and strength within, and not from ego-consciousness.

The more we live in the awareness of His presence, by daily concentration and meditation, the more surely we shall develop our own latent powers. Those powers, born of our attunement, can be used to overcome every difficulty we face.

Practice shooting burning smiles at the target of sorrowful hearts. Every time somebody's heart of sorrow is pierced with the bullet of your smile, you have "hit the bull's eye." Kill the blues with the blade of wisdom. As soon as you see a sorrowful heart, shoot into it sympathetic smiles and kind words. The minute you see somebody overcome with clouds of sorrow, disperse the clouds by the heavy, continuous cannonading of your courageous smiles.

When you see the gloom of hopelessness, shoot it at once with hope-awakening smiles. Do not form the habit of sorrowing, but form the habit of smiling. Make yourself adamant against taking offense, and freely forgive and forget those who offend you. Never get angry. Never allow yourself to become the victim of another's anger. Do your best to overcome difficulties, but smile first, last, and all the time. There is no better panacea for sorrow, no better reviving tonic, than smiles. There is no greater power with which to overcome failure than a real smile. There is no better ornament than a genuine smile. There is no beauty greater than the smile of peace and wisdom glowing on your face.

⁊᷁

O Silent Laughter, smile Thou through my soul. Let my soul smile through my heart, and let my heart smile through my eyes. O Prince of Smiles, be enthroned beneath the canopy of my countenance, and I will protect Thy tender Self in the castle of my sincerity, that no rebel hypocrisy may lurk to destroy Thee. Make me a Smile Millionaire, that I may scatter Thy smile in sad hearts freely, everywhere!

❧

Beginning with the early dawn, I will radiate my cheer to everyone I meet today. I will be the mental sunshine for all who cross my path this day.

❧

I will burn the candles of smiles in the bosom of the joyless. Before the unfading light of my cheer, darkness will take flight from the bosom of my brothers.

❧

Mother Divine, teach me to love others and to serve others. Teach me to be true to my word, even as I want others to be true to me. Teach me to love others as I wish them to love me. Teach me, O Mother, to make others happy — to make others smile. Teach me, O Mother, to find my happiness in the joy of others.

❧

CHAPTER 7

TRUE SUCCESS AND PROSPERITY

Millions of children are started on the path of life without a destination. They act like little toy engines, wound up with a little power, running without a track, only to smash up against anything that comes across their path. Such aimless journeys in life are the lot of most people, because in early life they were never started toward the right goal, nor were they properly equipped with systematic powers that would enable them to keep moving on their definite paths.

On this stage of life, most people act like puppet-actors, played by environment, prenatal instincts, and destiny. They never know what parts they can play successfully, nor can they harmonize their own duties with the general plan of the Cosmic Drama. Millions, so to say, do their duties in life as if in a somnambulistic state.

You should definitely discover your life's path, by analyzing early childhood and present life, before you hastily sidetrack in a wrong direction. Then, after you find your path, try to build around it all the creative moneymaking methods at your command. Your moneymaking methods, however, must be made within the boundaries of your idealism—otherwise, you may have money but not happiness. Happiness is only possible when the desire for making money cannot lure you to travel on the wrong path.

Wake up! It is never too late to diagnose your life. Analyze what you are and what your deep-seated work is, so that you can make yourself what you should be. You have talents and power that you have not used. You have all the power you need. There is nothing greater than the power of mind. Resurrect your mind from the little habits that keep you worldly. Smile that perpetual smile—the smile of God. Smile that strong smile of balanced recklessness, that billion dollar smile that no one can take from you.

✺

Swami Kriyananda writes the following:

A man burdened with worldly responsibilities asked, "What place does duty hold on the path to inner joy?"

Sri Yogananda replied: "To live irresponsibly is to live for the ego, not for God. The greater a person's emphasis on ego-fulfillment, the less his awareness of true joy.

"To fulfill one's duties in life may not be easy, and it may not always be immediately enjoyable. Attaining divine joy is a long-term proposition. Man must discharge his duties in life, and not avoid them, if he would attain freedom in eternity."

✺

Men of success are those who have nerve enough to make an indelible blueprint in their minds of whatever they wish to build or produce upon this earth. They then employ as the financiers their creative ability, as the builders their will power, as the carpenters their detailed attention, and as the laborers their mental patience—and thus materialize their dream.

You are unhappy because you do not visualize strongly enough the great things which you definitely want, nor do you employ your willpower, your creative ability, and your patience to materialize them. Happiness comes with your ability to manifest first your smallest desires, and later your biggest dreams.

You must be careful not to harbor impractical ambitions in your life and, consequently, spend your years wading through the mire of poverty and sarcasm from family and friends, as you chase a rainbow trail. Make mental blueprints of little things, and keep on making them materialize until you can make your big dreams also come true.

Be happy in the definite accomplishment of the small successes, and then you will know how to be a happiness millionaire when, later, you materialize the big dreams of your life. Unhappiness is caused by failure. You can create permanent happiness for yourself by letting nothing ever disturb you on your forward journey to success.

❧

There are no obstacles: There are only *opportunities!*

❧

Yogananda wrote the following essay to support Henry Ford's idea of replacing the six-day workweek with a five-day workweek:

Man is a spiritual and a material being. He ought to develop himself spiritually by inner discipline, but he must be materially efficient by developing his business faculties. Primitive man was busy using all his mental faculties for satisfying the needs of the material life. His time was spent in hunting, eating, and sleeping. Modern man scientifically tries to meet the present material conditions of life. What primitive man did unmethodically, modern man does methodically. This method in his efforts for material success has also, indirectly, improved his inner faculties.

The Masters of India believe in directly developing the inner faculties of will power to fight temptation, and of feeling for serving fellow beings.

Since God has given us hunger and since we have a physical body to look after, we must have money earned honestly and scientifically by serving the right needs of our fellow beings. Business life need not be a material life. Business ambition can be spiritualized. Business is nothing but serving others materially in the best possible way. People label those stores that start out with only the idea of making money, "moneymaking dens." But stores that concentrate wholly on serving customers with the best articles at a minimum cost are the ones that will always succeed and that will advance the moral development of the world.

I will never forget the remark of a fine salesman in a large shop where I was selecting an overcoat for myself. "Sir, I am not trying to sell you something. I am trying to find out exactly what you need." He knew I could buy a two hundred dollar overcoat, but he sold me a sixty-dollar one that exactly suited me. I was pleased to get what I needed at a reasonable price. He secured in me a permanent customer for his store. If he had sold me the costly overcoat, I would never have gone back there again.

In this way, people should spiritualize their business ambition by thinking of serving the proper needs of their fellow beings. Man should make money also for the sake of creating philanthropic institutions to serve public needs. When one makes a great deal of money by making others prosperous, and again uses that wealth for helping others to help themselves, that is spiritualizing ambition. Wealthy parents who leave too much money to their children choke the development of self-earned evolution, success, and happiness.

I agree with Mr. Henry Ford in helping people to help themselves and not in humiliating, slave-breeding charity. Only by having ambition crowned with the ideal of service will materially ambitious people find a spiritual reason for making money. Without ambition, we cripple our faculties, and thus hinder the progress of humanity.

One reason why Oriental peoples have been more spiritually inclined is because they have taken life more easily, refused to convert themselves into business automatons, and have had more time for contemplation. Of course, many Orientals used their leisure for feeding lazy habits instead of spiritual realization, but as a rule, the Oriental people have an awakened spiritual perception.

Our Western brothers have used their time in developing only the material and intellectual factors of life. They are too busy to enjoy the fruits even of their material labor, or to know much of peace, relaxation, and bliss. Many Western brothers are enslaved by their less important engagements and forget their highest engagement of blissful God-contact.

The Western brothers must make time. Though their struggle for a livelihood is greater, due to their colder climate, still, by their extensive use of machinery, they have an advantage over their Eastern brethren. They can thus save time to be used, less for dancing and amusements, and more for the deeper studies of life. Business activities and money are for the comfort of man, but blind greed for them must not rob him of his happiness.

Six full days and nights of machine-like existence, and part of one day only for spiritual culture, are not balanced. The week should be allotted to work, amusement, and spiritual culture—five days for making money, one day for rest and amusements, and one day for introspection and inner realization. Man must have some free time to find himself. One day a week—Sunday—is not enough, because it is his only holiday; he wants the day for rest and is too tired to meditate.

With a five-day work week, as proposed by Henry Ford, people could use Friday night, Saturday, and Sunday to get away from the noisy city environment and thus increase their longevity. The Chicago Chief of Police said that if city noises were eliminated, man's longevity could be increased by eleven years and his nervous system calmed down. Almost every family in America nowadays can afford an automobile and, with it, they can get out of the cities on weekends and refresh themselves in peaceful retreats in nature, living the double life of a hermit in the woods, and a warrior in the field of worldly activity.

It is extremely necessary that the five-day week of Henry Ford be carried out by all business concerns. Truth-loving, real-world patriots should cooperate by giving working people Saturday, a day for amusement and relaxation, and Sunday, an exclusive day for developing habits of meditation, seeking spiritual fellowship, and experiencing the highest good, the God-Bliss within.

The five-day working week plan is extremely desirable and necessary in order to give people more time to enjoy nature, simplify their lives, enjoy the true needs of their existence, get to know their children and friends better, and best of all, get to know *themselves*.

Why not learn the art of living rightly?

We must begin with children as well as with adults. The plastic mind of the child can be molded into any shape by self-disciplined adults. Desired habits can easily be created in children because their will to perform them is mostly free, except for a few innate tendencies. Adults have to battle and expel old habits in order to establish good ones. But all habits, whether in children or adults, must be cultivated through the medium of spontaneous willingness. In training children in a balanced life, or in habits of paying equal attention to the earning of money and to the acquisition of spiritual happiness, the time and method of training has to be considered.

People lose their balance and suffer from money madness and business madness only because they never had the opportunity to develop the habits of a balanced life. It is not our passing thoughts or brilliant ideas but our every-day habits that control our lives. There are some very busy businessmen who make millions without being unbalanced or nervous. There are other businessmen who become so engrossed in making money that they cannot think of anything else, and do not wake up until something terrible happens to them, such as sickness or loss of all happiness.

Many psychologists say that adult behavior is but the repetition of the training which one receives between the ages of two and ten or fifteen.

Spiritual sermons inspire the minds of children to better action, but that is all. Actual practical discipline for roasting the seeds of prenatal habits lodged in the subconscious and superconscious minds is necessary. This can only be done by scrubbing the brain cells of seed habits with the electricity of inner concentration. Children ought to be brought up with the spiritual ambition to make money only for the sake of service.

It lies in the hands of adults to uplift children and bring them into a balanced life. As long as adults remain intoxicated with a one-sided material life, children's highest potentials will remain unfulfilled.

Thus, in order to save the future world by saving the children, parents must wake up and cultivate balanced habits of material and spiritual life.

In order to lead a balanced life, adults must educate themselves and realize that business ambitions are only for making themselves and others happy. Without this realization, strenuous business activity only produces nervousness, greed for money, lack of social qualities, miserliness, and disrespect for all good principles. Only with this realization of service for others can life be really happy.

I know many prominent, intelligent businessmen who in their heart of hearts are discontented with everything and are craving God and wisdom, but they are helplessly carried away by their habits and too many engagements. They sacrifice their highest engagement with God, Truth, higher studies, and more home life for moneymaking or some useless engagement.

As the art of war needs certain training, so does our battle with active life need certain training. Untrained warriors are soon killed on the battlefield; so also, men untrained in the art of preserving their poise and peace are quickly riddled by the bullets of worry and restlessness in active life.

Very few people analyze whether they are progressing or going backward in life. As human beings endowed with reason, wisdom, and understanding, it is our greatest duty to use our reason and wisdom rightly so that we may know whether we are going backward or forward.

If failures trouble you repeatedly, don't get discouraged. They should act as stimulants, not poisons, to your material or spiritual growth. The period of failure is the best season for sowing the seeds of success. Weed out the causes of failure and launch with double vigor what you want to accomplish.

The bludgeon of circumstances may bleed you, but keep your head unbowed. Death in the attempt to succeed is success; refuse to harbor the consciousness of defeat. Always try once more, no matter how many times you have failed. Persevere *one minute more* in the race for success when you have done your best and can do no more. Fight when you think that you can fight no more, or when you think that you have fought your best.

Every new effort after a failure must be well planned and charged with increasing intensity of attention. Begin from today to try to do one thing at a time, the things you thought impossible for you to do.

⁂

Change is often approached with apprehension. In giving up something, people think, Will I be left with nothing? It takes courage to renounce the known for the unknown. It is not easy even to renounce a familiar pain for an unknown, and therefore uncertain, happiness. The mind is like a horse that for years has pulled its delivery wagon. The horse is accustomed to its daily route, and cannot be convinced easily to walk a new one. The mind, too, will not lightly abandon its old habits, even when it knows they cause only misery.

Beneficial changes should be embraced with courage. As long as one's hopes for better things are opposed by fear of their attainment, the mind can never be at peace. Accept change, therefore, as life's only constant. Our lives are an endless procession of gains and losses, of joys and sorrows, of hopes and disappointments. At one moment we find ourselves threatened by the storms of trials; moments later, a silver lining brightens the gray clouds; then, suddenly, the skies are blue again.

Life is change.

Remain ever calm within. Be even-minded. When working, be calmly active. Someday, you will know yourself to be subject no longer to the tides of destiny. Your strength will come from within; you will not depend on outer incentives of any kind for motivation.

As a devotee on the spiritual path, give little weight to the trials that beset you. Be even-minded. Walk with courage. Go forward from day to day with calm, inner faith. Eventually, you will pass beyond every shadow of bad karma, beyond all tests and difficulties, and will behold at last the dawn of divine fulfillment. In that highest of all states of consciousness will come freedom from every last, trailing vapor of misfortune.

❧

To help your family with food is necessary, but to help them develop their mental powers is more necessary. To help develop their souls by leading them to meditative ways of God-contact is of paramount importance.

❧

You must do something every day to satisfy the Cosmic Plan for which you were sent here. Most people are unhappy because they forget to harmonize their earthly, learned duties with their duties according to the demands of the Cosmic

Plan. The Cosmic Plan demands that you include in your true happiness the happiness of the most needy ones, if you would satisfy your soul.

Every day try to help uplift those physically, mentally, or spiritually sick as you would help yourself or your family. If, from today, instead of living in the old misery-making selfish way, you live scientifically according to the laws of mind and of God, then, no matter what little part you may be playing on the stage of life, you will know that you have been playing your part well, as directed by the Stage Manager of all our destinies. And remember, your part, however small, is just as important as the biggest parts in contributing to the entire success of the Drama of Souls on the stage of Life. Make a little money and be satisfied with it by living a simple life and expressing your ideals, rather than have lots of money and worries without end.

∞

Trials do not come to you to destroy you, but in order that you may appreciate God better. God does not send those trials; they are of your own making. All you have to do is to resurrect your consciousness from the environment of ignorance. Environmental troubles are born because of your conscious or unconscious actions in the past, somewhere, sometime. We must blame ourselves for that. However, you must not develop an inferiority complex. You must say: "I know that Thou art coming! I shall see Thy silver lining, and in this tumultuous sea of trials Thou art the polestar of my shipwrecked thoughts.' Why are you afraid? Remember, you are not a man or a woman. You are not what you think you are. You are an immortal being.

Habits are your deadliest enemies. Even as Jesus could manifest His love and say, when sorely tested: "Father, forgive them, for they know not what they do," so you must forgive your exacting trials and say: "My soul is resurrected. My power is greater than all my trials because I am the child of God." Thus, your mental powers will expand, and your cup of realization will be big enough to hold the Ocean of Knowledge. Your forever-hungry desires must be attended to, and nourished with proper environment and activity. Then you will be happy and prosperous.

❧

Most people reason that if they first have prosperity, then they can think of God, but you must have God *first* because He is what you need. If *that* consciousness comes, then you will have real happiness. God must be with you always. If you once have that great contact with God, then the prosperity of the universe will absolutely be at your feet. So, don't forget that God is your provider. It isn't what you own, but what you can get at will, that is real prosperity.

To live a contradictory life is to live unspiritually. When your whole consciousness, no matter what your faults are, is toward God, toward the silence, then that is being with God. When you perform all the duties of life cheerfully, without letting any duties upset your happiness, that is called "spiritual happiness." That is when all your mind and consciousness is going back toward the source—toward God, freedom, fresh air, happiness, and plain living. These are the highest things that the Masters of India teach. The Masters have always given the training of plain living and high thinking to students.

You are living directly by the power of God. Suppose God suddenly changed the climate of this country. What then? Where would be the food? How would you live? Why not remember that God is the supporter of the life that He gave to you? Even though He made that life dependent upon food, still He is the direct support. He is the Cause of everything, so when you lose your connection with God you are bound to suffer.

To forget God and live buried in luxury is heathenish. "Having little, I have everything, for I have God." Yogis have learned that God can never be found outside, but when you go deep within your soul, in the temple of God, then you can say: "No one in the whole world cares for my health, prosperity, and happiness as my Father does. He is with me always."

❦

Every day affirm: "Lord, Thou art my provider. Manifest Thy prosperity through me. Father, Thou art my riches; I am rich. Thou art the owner of all things. I am Thy child. I have what Thou hast." You should affirm this before going to work in the morning. Remember that you are absolutely living by God's laws, and He will show you the way. Man showed you the way and then left you cold. God's way will bring you happiness and prosperity.

If we can come to that state when we can say: "What is mine is Yours," then it will be much better. It is extremely difficult in this age of selfishness to be prosperous. Selfishness must go. It can only be destroyed by everyone being unselfish. You must live it yourself. And the best way to teach is by your own example.

Although it is necessary to make money, it is more necessary to gain happiness. Money is made for happiness and not happiness made for money. Those who concentrate upon making money as their only happiness do not find real satisfaction, for no amount of money can buy happiness if it is lost through systematic wrong actions.

People surrounded with money but unable to use it properly in order to make themselves and others happy, die of happiness thirst. Many people forget that making money is only a means to the goal of happiness. It is as ridiculous to concentrate upon the means and forget the goal as it is to keep traveling on a road and forget your destination. It is meaningless to develop the habit of accumulating money and not use it to make yourself and others happy.

Many people make the mistake of running after money first instead of first seeking happiness. To try to earn money with a disgruntled, worried mind is not only unsuccessful, but it produces more anxiety and unhappiness. The best way lies in trying to make money after first making sure of happiness. Earning money with a serene and happy attitude leads not only to success but ensures happiness also. Happy people make others happy by their example, for actions speak louder than words.

※

Some people say that happiness is found only in mental contentment, whereas others say it consists in having lots of money, an over-abundance of furniture, yachts, estates, and cars. Both these views are one-sided and incomplete.

The ascetic, sitting in a cave, may have some mental contentment, but he has to depend upon food products grown by a farmer or produced by a factory. He has to wear clothing made by a weaver. No ascetic in the world could find complete happiness only in the mind, without the use of at least a few material things.

On the other hand, it is untrue that all happiness is dependent upon constantly buying the countless objects that one's fancy may dictate. In fact, when happiness is sought only through the acquisition of an infinite number of material things, it can never be found, for happiness consists principally in the attitude of the mind, and is conditioned only partially by outside factors.

There have been martyrs who sacrificed their lives rather than lose the inner comforts of their minds. Such people have found happiness in states of the mind without the addition of any material things. On the other hand, it is very rare to find people happy who seek happiness only by acquiring more and more material objects.

The man whose entire happiness is dependent upon the creation and fulfillment of new desires can never be happy, for his happiness is always dependent upon something that he expects to have sometime in the future. He courts happiness without ever winning it, just as a dog will chase continually after the ever-receding sausage, dangling far-off in front of his eyes, from the end of a long stick tied on his back.

Man can never satisfy his desires if he forgets that happiness is mostly in the mind, and only partially in the acquisition of the world's necessities.

☙

Remember that he who seeks only material pleasures will lose the divine joys hidden behind them. He that finds the cosmic joy of meditation loses the attachment to the pleasures of material life. He who loses the desire for material pleasures in order to find the Christ Intelligence within will find the everlasting joys hidden behind material life.

That devotee who forgoes the pleasure of the body to feel the ever-new joy felt in ecstasy in meditation will find that all material prosperity and pleasures of earthly life will be added unto him. He who forsakes earthly happiness for God happiness will find earthly happiness, too, but he who seeks material happiness only will lose it because of its short-lasting nature.

❦

Bless me, that I may perceive Thee through the windows of all joyous activities. Mayest Thou look at me and cheer me always, while I am engaged in my duties. Let my every activity—waking, sleeping, dreaming—be sprayed with Thy Presence.

Father, teach me to perform every work just to please Thee. Let me feel that Thou art the electricity of my life, which moves the machinery of my bones, nerves, and muscles. In every heart-throb, every breath, every outburst of vital activity, teach me to feel Thy Power.

❦

CHAPTER 8

INNER FREEDOM AND JOY

Swami Kriyananda shares the following story:

"If I had no desires," asked a congregation member, "wouldn't I lose all motivation, and become a sort of automaton?"

"Many people imagine so," Yogananda replied. "They think they'd have no further interest in life. But that isn't what happens at all. Rather, you would find life to be infinitely more interesting.

"Consider the negative aspect of desire. It keeps you forever fearful. 'What if this happens?' you think; or, 'What if that doesn't happen?' You live in a state of anxiety for the future, or of regret for the past.

"Non-attachment, on the other hand, helps you to live perpetually in a state of inner freedom and happiness. When you can be happy in the present, then you have God.

"Desirelessness doesn't rob you of motivation. Far from it! The more you live in God, the deeper the joy you experience in serving Him."

❧

If you aspire to wisdom and unalloyed happiness, keep the feelings of your heart free. Don't over-react to life's ups and downs. Don't, in other words, when fortune visits you, dive boisterously into sparkling streams of excitement. Resist the temptation to sink despondently into a bog of despair when the trail before you suggests no way out of present difficulties.

For the unwary, the material world is an uncharted wilderness, fraught with peril. Occasional success—whether one's own or someone else's—lures the unpracticed hiker down countless trails of false hope. Too often, alas, the path vanishes into a desert of broken dreams. Success alternates with failure, like ridges and valleys on a mountain range.

The rules for a fruitful, happy life are not many, nor are they difficult to follow. They must, however, be studied carefully, by putting them into daily practice.

Toil and struggle are the norms of life on earth. They are blessings, not misfortunes, for they provide us with a testing ground for our own inner development. As we hone our peace of mind—its pure metal forged in meditation—on the abrasive surface of outer difficulties, we develop the clear discrimination with which to slice through to delusion's heart. Eventually we arrive at that blessed state where the very luster of our peace protects us during all our activities.

The most important condition for lasting happiness is even-mindedness. Remain ever calmly centered in the Self, within. As a child's sand castle disintegrates before invading waves, so does a restless mind, lacking strength of will and perseverance, succumb to the pounding it receives from the waves of changing circumstance.

A diamond, however, retains its strength and clarity no matter how many waves crash down upon it. The man of inner peace, similarly, his consciousness made crystalline by inner calmness, retains his equanimity through even the storms of mighty trials.

A good rule in life is to tell yourself simply, "Whatever comes of itself, let it come."

Life will bring you many ups and downs. If you let your feelings rise and fall with the waves of circumstance, you will never attain that inner calmness which is the foundation of spiritual progress. Be careful, therefore, not to react emotionally. Rise above likes and dislikes.

A good rule to live by, and one that will take you sailing through many tests in life, is, under all circumstances, to remain *even-minded and cheerful.*

Be neither elated nor depressed at anything outside yourself. Behold the passing spectacle of life with an even mind. For life's ups and downs are but waves on an ocean, constantly in flux. Shun emotional involvement with them, while remaining ever calm, ever happy at your inner center in the spine.

The end result of emotional extremes is extreme emotional dissatisfaction. Perfect happiness lies not at any of the extremities of outer experiences, but at a point of calmness midway between them all.

Let not your possessions possess *you*, nor the petty details of worldly life invade with hordes of worry the stillness of your heart.

The wave protruding from the ocean bosom is still a part of the ocean. This is God's body. If He wants to make it well, all right. If He wants to keep it unwell, all right. It is best to remain impartial. If you have health and are attached to it, you will always be afraid of losing it. And if you are attached to good health and become ill, you will be always grieving for the good that you have lost.

Man's greatest trouble is egoism, the consciousness of individuality. He takes everything that happens to him as affecting *him*, personally. Why be affected? You are not this body. You are *He!* Everything is Spirit.

❧

Objective conditions are always neutral. It is how you react to them that makes them appear sad or happy.

Work on yourself: on your reactions to outer circumstances. This is the essence of yoga: to neutralize the waves of reaction in the heart. Be ever happy inside. You will never be able to change things outwardly in such a way as to make them ever pleasing to you.

Change yourself.

❧

It requires only shallow wisdom to be disillusioned with life. World-weary metaphysicians pride themselves on their "aloofness from it all," and turn up their noses at a 180-degree angle at the mere mention of anything beautiful. Granted, life is riddled with inconsistencies. Earthly fulfillments are, in fact, short lasting. Recognition of these realities is not, in itself, any proof of profundity. Nothing of value is ever attained by negativity alone.

Wisdom must be approached with a positive outlook. Why sneer at the world? Accept, rather, the pure joy you feel in outer stimuli and feed it into the soul's joy, within. Use outer happiness as a reminder of the inner heaven. This inward absorption of sense stimuli actually increases the joy felt in outward experiences, for it reinforces joy at its true source.

Be neither elated nor depressed at anything outside yourself. Behold the passing spectacle of life with an even mind. For life's ups and downs are but waves on an ocean, constantly in flux. Shun emotional involvement with them, while remaining ever calm, ever happy, at your inner center in the spine.

World-weariness—the metaphysician's dour alternative to emotional excitement—is inadequate as a cure for life's sufferings, for it fosters an attitude of indifference, the progenitor of spiritual laziness.

Neither brood, then, on life's disappointments, nor yet revel in its fleeting victories. Trust not in riches, but, on the other hand, don't spurn contemptuously life's generous bounty. Nurture your high, spiritual potentials, taking care only not to scatter them in worthless pursuits.

See God's changeless beauty at the heart of change, and in every good thing. Seek, above all, that which the wise have: God-consciousness, immortality in Him. Release into the Infinite every attachment—even the least of them. Let the world shout in outrage, or leap up and down in a hysteria of false joy. What matters it? It is all a parade—entertaining, colorful, but for all that only a parade, passing endlessly.

☙

CHAPTER 9

FINDING GOD IS THE GREATEST HAPPINESS

The purpose of human life is to find God. That is the only reason for our existence. Job, friends, material interests — these things in themselves mean nothing. They can never provide you with true happiness, for the simple reason that none of them, in itself, is complete. Only God encompasses everything.

That is why Jesus said, "Seek ye first the kingdom of God, and all these things shall be added unto you." (Matthew 6:33) Seek ye first the Giver of all gifts, and you shall receive from Him all His gifts of lesser fulfillment.

※

Joy is an aspect of God. Divine joy is like millions of earthly joys crushed into one. The quest for human happiness is like looking around for a candle while sitting out of doors in the sun. Divine joy surrounds us eternally, yet people look to mere things for their happiness. Mostly, all they find is relief from emotional or physical pain. But divine joy is the blazing Reality. Before it, earthly joys are but shadows.

※

Pray thus to God:

"My Infinite Beloved, I know that Thou art nearer than these words with which I pray; nearer even than my nearest thoughts. Behind my every restless feeling, may I feel Thy concern for me, and Thy love. Behind my awareness, may I feel sustained and guided by Thy consciousness. Behind my love for Thee, may I become ever more deeply conscious of Thy love."

If you continuously pray to Him in this way, and if you pray with all sincerity, you will feel His presence suddenly as a great joy in your heart. In that bursting joy you will know that He is with you, and that He is your very own.

The true purpose of life is to know God. Worldly temptations were given you to help you develop discrimination: Will you prefer sense pleasures, or will you choose God? Pleasures seem alluring at first, but if you choose them, sooner or later you will find yourself enmeshed in endless troubles and difficulties.

Loss of health, of peace of mind, and of happiness is the lot of everyone who succumbs to the lure of sense pleasures. Infinite joy, on the other hand, is yours once you know God.

Every human being will have, eventually, to learn this great lesson of life.

❦

Suffering is a reminder that this world is not our home. If it were perfect for us, how many people would seek a better one? Even with things as imperfect as they are, see how few people seek God! Out of a thousand, said Krishna, perhaps one.

The law of life is this: The less one lives in harmony with the truth within, the more he suffers; but the more he lives in harmony with that truth, the more he experiences unending happiness. Nothing then can touch him, even though his body waste away with disease and people ridicule and persecute him. Through all the vagaries of life, he remains ever blissfully centered in the indwelling Self.

❦

"Get away," Krishna said, "from My ocean of suffering and misery!" With God, life is a feast of happiness, but without Him it is a nest of troubles, pains, and disappointments.

Deep meditation keeps the consciousness always on God, and lack of meditation keeps the consciousness on the senses. If you are not meditating and you still feel a nearness to God all the time, you are retaining the full benefit of your recent meditation. If you can retain the joy and thrill of meditation during the entire day, you are still meditating. You are then unattached to the senses. When you can feel God in the flesh as well as in meditation, it is complete. That is what devotees who follow the path of meditation experience. They become detached; they do everything as a part of their duty but are not attached to it.

Occasionally, a soul realizes the joy that is in meditation and searches for God day and night; even when God doesn't answer, still he goes on until suddenly he finds God. We have to work to reach the Infinite, and work in the right way. No one can give you Self-realization. You have to work for that reward. All the spiritual teachers in the world cannot give you salvation unless you make the effort to receive it.

Joy and God are one. Joy is the healing that you want first, the healing of the ignorance of the soul. Eventually you will have to dump the physical body in the dust, so you must think of Spirit now. Affirmations are better than the usual form of prayers. Do not beg favors from God. He will not break any law of His universe because you ask Him to, but when you demand your birthright as a child of His, then He will listen. A long prayer with words, words, words, does not mean anything at all, for then the mind is wandering. Doing an affirmation, one should both say and feel deeply the meaning of the thought behind the words; then the thought will go deeply into the conscious mind, then into the subconscious, and then into the superconscious. When it registers in the superconsciousness, it manifests.

Always affirm with intelligence and devotion until your thought goes consciously through the subconscious mind into the superconscious mind. The greatest healing you should pray for is the healing of your ignorance, so that you will never go back to your old life. The best and highest reward in our life is the realization of unceasing happiness, which we call peace, or bliss.

❧

If one loses a diamond and tries to satisfy himself with little pieces of broken glass, shining with sunlight, he is bound to be disillusioned. He cannot find the diamond in the pile of broken glass. He is seeking in the wrong place and can never be happy until he seeks in the right place and finds the diamond. In the same way, the soul tries to find its happiness in the momentarily glittering sense-pleasures, but when it has enough of sense-happiness it becomes disgusted and tries to find peace and joy in the soul.

It is foolish to expect true happiness from material things, for they are powerless to give it, and yet, millions of people die of broken hearts trying vainly to find the comfort in material things which God alone can impart.

The soul, being individualized Spirit, if given a chance to unfold, can manifest all the fulfillment and satisfaction of the Spirit. It is through long-continued contact with changeable matter that material desires are developed.

Protect the soul from the disturbance created within your mind by the mad dance of sorrow-producing desire. Learn to overcome wild, wicked desire. Realize that you do not need the things which create misery, for if you search within your soul you will find there true happiness and lasting peace, or bliss. Thus you will become a "bliss billionaire."

The soul's nature is bliss—a lasting, inner state of ever-new, ever-changing joy which eternally entertains, even when one passes through the trials of physical suffering or death. Desirelessness is not a negation; it is rather the attainment of the self-control you need in order to regain the heritage of all-fulfillment lying within your soul.

First, give the soul the opportunity to manifest this state, by meditation. Then, constantly living in this state, do your duty to your body and mind and the world. You need not give up your ambitions and become negative; on the contrary, let the ever-lasting joy, which is your true nature, help you to realize all noble ambitions. Enjoy noble experiences with the joy of God. Perform real duties with divine joy.

You are immortals, endowed with eternal joy. Never forget this during your play with changeable mortal life. This world is but a stage on which you play your parts under the direction of the Divine Stage Manager. Play them well, whether they be tragic or comic, always remembering that your real nature is eternal bliss, and nothing else. The one thing that will never leave you is the joy of your soul.

Therefore, learn to swim in the calm sea of unchanging bliss before you attempt to plunge into the maelstrom of material life that is the realm of sorrow, pleasure, indifference, and a deceptive, temporary peace.

The whole-hearted practice of meditation brings deep bliss. This ever-new bliss is not born of desire; it manifests itself by the magic command of your inner, intuition-born calmness. Manifest this serenity always. When bliss comes over you, you will recognize it as a conscious, intelligent, universal Being to whom you may appeal, and not as an abstract mental state. This is the surest proof that God is eternal, ever-conscious, ever-new bliss.

⚜

Keep your expectations of life positive. Strive to live with unceasing happiness. Let not your possessions possess you, nor the petty details of worldly life invade with hordes of worry the stillness of your heart. Gain strength to rise above distraction by sipping frequently the nectar of inner peace, given you lovingly by angel hands as you grow silently toward Self-realization.

⚜

The wise, even if blessed with material prosperity, never lose sight of the truth that all things are evanescent.

Fools, who look to this imperfect world for fulfillment, never gain from it more than fleeting satisfaction. For the very fairest and most delicate dream of earthly happiness cannot but join the solemn procession that winds its way toward the crematory ground of disillusionment.

The wise understand life's fleeting nature. They waste no time in building dream-castles of futile expectations. Instead, they cultivate non-attachment to this earth's experiences. When death comes, they find the perfection of fulfillment in God.

❧

Why are you still sleeping?! Offer no excuses to yourself that you are too busy to think of God! When death comes, you will have to leave all your engagements at once without notice or delay. Then why not now give up some of your useless pursuits and idle thoughts to make time for God?

The world takes from you all it can, and keeps you engaged with worthless habits and unproductive activities. You may wish to be different, but day after day you are a prisoner, bound hand and foot by the cord of your habits. You are responsible for yourself, and the world will not answer for your deeds. Then why not remember each day, "My most important engagement is with God"?

To eat, work, and die is not enough; the animal does the same. Use your precious gift of reason and try to find Him. You do not need to go to the forest, where other, different temptations will assail and conquer you. Your work is in the world, where your karma has placed you to work out your salvation by serving your fellow man.

You can find God in the solitude of your own room when, in the early morning hours and before sleeping, you compose yourself for meditation. With folded hands say mentally, "Father, Thou art omniscient. Thou knowest my every thought. Talk to me. I want to hear Thy voice." Say it mentally again and again until you feel it. You have to culture this feeling, to work for it. Repeat the prayer again and again until you find your heart throbs with love and yearning for God, and you get a conscious response.

Whenever you find yourself with a few moments of leisure, make a sincere prayer, "Father, come to me, reveal Thine omniscient presence." Let no one know of your secret prayers. And remember, you cannot know God if other desires are in your mind at the same time. "Thou shalt have no other gods before Me" means God will not reveal Himself to you if your thoughts for Him are not strong enough to blot out all distracting thoughts.

When you wish to express your love for someone, you do not need to quote from a book of poems to express that love. Your love finds its own words, which flow spontaneously from the awakened heart. So pray to God mostly in your own words of love and yearning, not in the borrowed language of others. Never cease to keep up your prayers to God until He answers you.

Act from today onward on your desire to know God. Make the effort *now* to cultivate His friendship, without ignoring your worldly duties, but with the thought that you are realizing Him through those duties and thus are pleasing Him.

INDEX

Further Explorations

If you are inspired by *How to Be Happy All the Time* and would like to learn more about Paramhansa Yogananda and his teachings, Crystal Clarity Publishers offers many additional resources to assist you:

Autobiography of a Yogi

Paramhansa Yogananda

This is a new edition, featuring previously unavailable material, of a true spiritual classic, **Autobiography of a Yogi**: one of the best-selling eastern philosophy titles of all-time, with millions of copies sold, named one of the best and most influential books of the 20th century.

This highly prized verbatim reprinting of the original 1946 edition is the **ONLY** one available free from textual changes made after Yogananda's death.

This updated edition contains bonus materials, including a last chapter that Yogananda himself wrote in 1951, five years after the publication of the first edition. It is the only version of this chapter available without posthumous changes.

Yogananda was the first yoga master of India whose mission it was to live and teach in the West. His first-hand account of his life experiences includes childhood revelations, stories of his visits to saints and masters in India, and long-secret teachings of Self-realization that he made available to the Western reader.

There are two different collections of the sayings, stories, and wisdom of Yogananda, each covering a diverse range of spiritual practices and topics, presented in an enjoyable, easy-to-read format.

Conversations with Yogananda

Edited with commentary by Swami Kriyananda

This is an unparalleled, first-hand account of the teachings of Paramhansa Yogananda. Featuring nearly 500 never-before-released stories, sayings, and insights, this is an extensive, yet eminently accessible treasure trove of wisdom from one of the 20th Century's most famous yoga masters. Compiled and edited with commentary, by Swami Kriyananda, one of Yogananda's closest direct disciples.

The Essence of Self-Realization

Edited and compiled by Swami Kriyananda

A fantastic volume of the stories, sayings, and wisdom of Paramhansa Yogananda, this book covers more than 20 essential topics about the spiritual path and practices. Subjects covered include: the true purpose of life, the folly of materialism, the essential unity of all religions, the laws of karma and reincarnation, grace vs. self-effort, the need for a guru, how to pray effectively, meditation, and many more.

If you'd like a succinct, easy-to-understand overview of Yogananda's teachings and their place within ancient and contemporary spiritual thought and practices, we suggest:

God Is for Everyone

Inspired by Paramhansa Yogananda, written by Swami Kriyananda

This book outlines the core of Yogananda's teachings. *God Is for Everyone* presents a concept of God and spiritual meaning that will broadly appeal to everyone, from the most uncertain agnostic to the most fervent believer. Clearly and simply written, thoroughly nonsectarian and non-dogmatic in its approach, with a strong emphasis on the underlying unity of all religions, this is the perfect introduction to the spiritual path.

During his lifetime, Yogananda was famous for being a powerful speaker and riveting personality, and an awe-inspiring presence. If you'd like to experience a taste of this, we suggest:

Paramhansa Yogananda: Rare Film Collection

This DVD contains three short film clips of the world-renowned spiritual teacher, Paramhansa Yogananda, recorded in the 1920s and 1930s. Thrilling and utterly riveting, the unique combination of both seeing and hearing Yogananda is a life-changing experience. Also included is a video slideshow depicting many of the places that Yogananda himself wrote about in *Autobiography of a Yogi*. Narrated by his close disciple, Swami Kriyananda, this video retraces Yogananda's footsteps throughout India, recounting his visits with many great saints and sages. Filled with many rare and precious photographs. This is a must-have for anyone who has ever been touched by this great master.

Yogananda has many direct disciples, individuals that he personally trained to carry-on various aspects of his mission after his passing. One of the best known of these disciples is Swami Kriyananda, the founder of Ananda and

Crystal Clarity Publishers. Kriyananda's autobiography, a sequel of sorts to *Autobiography of a Yogi*, contains hundreds of stories about Yogananda, culled from the nearly four years that Kriyananda lived with and was trained by Yogananda. It offers the unique perspective of a disciple reflecting on his time with a great Master:

The Path
One Man's Quest on the Only Path There Is
Swami Kriyananda (J. Donald Walters)

The Path is the moving story of Kriyananda's years with Paramhansa Yogananda. *The Path* completes Yogananda's life story and includes more than 400 never-before-published stories about Yogananda, India's emissary to the West and the first yoga master to spend the greater part of his life in America.

If you would like to learn more about the spiritual heritage of India, the highest meaning of Hinduism, Yoga, and Christianity, including the deeper, underlying unity between Eastern and Western spirituality, you will enjoy reading:

The Hindu Way of Awakening

Its Revelation, Its Symbols: An Essential View of Religion

Swami Kriyananda

In a scholarly and thorough manner, Kriyananda brings order to the seeming chaos of the vast symbols and imagery one encounters in Hinduism, and clearly communicates the underlying teachings from which these symbols arise. Sure to deepen your understanding and appreciation of the Hindu religion, this book also helps establish the transcendent unity of all religions.

The Promise of Immortality

The True Teaching of the Bible and the Bhagavad

J. Donald Walters (Swami Kriyananda)

Destined to become a classic, *The Promise of Immortality* is the most complete commentary available on the parallel passages in the Bible and the Bhagavad Gita, India's ancient scripture. Compellingly written, this groundbreaking book illuminates the similarities between these two great scriptures in a way that vibrantly brings them to life. Mr. Walters sheds light on famous passages from both texts, showing their practical relevance for the modern day, and their potential to help us achieve lasting spiritual transformation.

If you would like to learn how to begin your own practice of yoga postures, meditation, Kriya Yoga, and more, as taught by Yogananda and Kriyananda, we strongly recommend the following:

The Art and Science of Raja Yoga
Swami Kriyananda

Contains fourteen lessons in which the original yoga science emerges in all its glory—a proven system for realizing one's spiritual destiny. This is the most comprehensive course available on yoga and meditation today. Over 450 pages of text and photos give you a complete and detailed presentation of yoga postures, yoga philosophy, affirmations, meditation instruction, and breathing techniques. Also included are suggestions for daily yoga routines, information on proper diet, recipes, and alternative healing techniques. The book also comes with an audio CD that contains: a guided yoga postures sessions, a guided meditation, and an inspiring talk on how you can use these techniques to solve many of the problems of daily life.

Meditation for Starters

J. Donald Walters (Swami Kriyananda)

Meditation brings balance into our lives, providing an oasis of profound rest and renewal. Doctors are prescribing it for a variety of stress-related diseases. This award-winning book offers simple but powerful guidelines for attaining inner peace. Learn to prepare the body and mind for meditation with special breathing techniques and ways to focus and "let go"; develop superconscious awareness; strengthen your willpower; improve your intuition and increase your calmness.

Ananda Yoga for Higher Awareness

Swami Kriyananda (J. Donald Walters)

Ananda Yoga is the system of postures that Kriyananda developed based on the training and instruction he personally received from Yogananda. This handy lay-flat reference book covers the basic principles of hatha yoga, including relaxation poses, spinal stretches, and inverted and sitting poses, all illustrated with photographs. Includes suggestions for routines of varying lengths for beginning to advanced study.

Affirmations for Self-Healing

J. Donald Walters (Swami Kriyananda)

This inspirational book contains 52 affirmations and prayers, each pair devoted to improving a quality in ourselves. Strengthen your will power; cultivate forgiveness, patience, health, and enthusiasm. A powerful tool for self-transformation.

Crystal Clarity also makes available many music and spoken word audio resources. Here are some that you might find helpful:

Kriyananda Chants Yogananda

Swami Kriyananda

This CD offers a rare treat: hear Swami Kriyananda chant the spiritualized songs of his guru, Paramhansa Yogananda, in a unique and deeply inward way. Throughout the ages, chanting has been a means to achieve deeper meditation. Kriyananda's devotional chanting is certain to uplift your spirit.

AUM: Mantra of Eternity

Swami Kriyananda

This recording features nearly 70 minutes of continuous vocal chanting of Aum, the Sanskrit word meaning peace and oneness of spirit. Aum, the cosmic creative vibration, is extensively discussed by Yogananda in *Autobiography of a Yogi*. Chanted here by his disciple, Kriyananda, this recording is a stirring way to tune into this cosmic power.

Mantra

Swami Kriyananda

Discover the ancient healing chants of India. For millennia, the Gayatri Mantra and the Mahamrityunjaya Mantra have echoed down the banks of the holy river Ganges. These mantras express the heart's longing for peace, wisdom, and ultimate freedom from all earthly limitations, expressing the essence of every prayer. Both mantras are chanted in the traditional Sanskrit style, accompanied by the sound of 120 tambouras.

Metaphysical Meditations

Swami Kriyananda (J. Donald Walters)

Kriyananda's soothing voice leads you in thirteen guided meditations based on the soul-inspiring, mystical poetry of Paramhansa Yogananda. Each meditation is accompanied by beautiful classical music to help you quiet your thoughts and prepare you for deep states of meditation. Includes a full recitation of Yogananda's poem, Samadhi, which appears in *Autobiography of a Yogi*. A great aid to the serious meditator, as well as those just beginning their practice.

This edition of *Autobiography of a Yogi* is also available as an audio book.

Autobiography of a Yogi

by Paramhansa Yogananda, read by Swami Kriyananda

audio book, selected chapters, 10 hours

This is a recording of the original, unedited 1946 edition of *Autobiography of a Yogi*, presented on six cassettes. Read by Swami Kriyananda, this is the only audio edition that is read by one of Yogananda's direct disciples—someone who both knew him and was directly trained by him. This abridged reading focuses on the key chapters and most thrilling sections of this spiritual classic.

Crystal Clarity Publishers

Crystal Clarity Publishers offers many additional resources to assist you in your spiritual journey including many other books, a wide variety of inspirational and relaxation music composed by Swami Kriyananda, and yoga and meditation videos.

To request a catalog, place an order for the above products, or to find out more information, please contact us at:

Crystal Clarity Publishers
14618 Tyler Foote Rd.
Nevada City, CA 95959
800.424.1055 or 530.478.7600
Fax: 530.478.7610
clarity@crystalclarity.com

For our online catalog, complete with secure ordering, please visit us on the web at:
www.crystalclarity.com

Ananda Worldwide

Ananda Sangha, a worldwide organization founded by Swami Kriyananda, offers spiritual support and resources based on the teachings of Paramhansa Yogananda. There are Ananda spiritual communities in Nevada City, Sacramento, and Palo Alto (CA), Seattle, Portland (OR), and Hopkinton, RI, as well as a retreat center and European community in Assisi, Italy and a center and community near New Delhi, India. Ananda supports more than 75 meditation groups worldwide.

For more information about Ananda Sangha, communities, or meditation groups near you, please contact:

530.478.7560

www.ananda.org

The Expanding Light

Ananda's guest retreat, The Expanding Light, offers a varied, year round schedule of classes and workshops on yoga, meditation, and spiritual practice. You may also come for a relaxed personal renewal, participating in ongoing activities as much or as little as you wish.

The beautiful serene mountain setting, supportive staff, and delicious vegetarian food provide an ideal environment for a truly meaningful, spiritual vacation.

For more information, please contact:

800.346.5350

www.expandinglight.org